The Spirit of Christmas

The Spirit of Christmas

Copyright © 2013 Lire Classics

by Henry Van Dyke

Published originally by Charles Scribner's Sons, New York; 1909.

All rights reserved. No part of this book may be reproduced in any form by any electronic or mechanical means including photocopying, recording, or information storage and retrieval without permission in writing from the author.

ISBN-10: 1939652456
ISBN-13: 978-1-939652-45-4

Lire Classics is an imprint of Lire Books LCC.

Book Website
www.LireBooks.com
Email: contact@LireBooks.com

Give feedback on the book at:
feedback@LireBooks.com

Printed in U.S.A

THE SPIRIT OF CHRISTMAS

By Henry Van Dyke

Lire Classics: New York

Contents

A DREAM-STORY

    The Christmas Angel 11

A LITTLE ESSAY

    Christmas-Giving and Christmas-Living 29

A SHORT CHRISTMAS SERMON

    Keeping Christmas 37

TWO CHRISTMAS PRAYERS

    A Christmas Prayer for the Home 43

    A Christmas Prayer for Lonely Folks 48

A Dream-Story

The Christmas Angel

It was the hour of rest in the Country Beyond the Stars. All the silver bells that swing with the turning of the great ring of light which lies around that land were softly chiming; and the sound of their commotion went down like dew upon the golden ways of the city, and the long alleys of blossoming trees, and the meadows of asphodel, and the curving shores of the River of Life.

At the hearing of that chime, all the angels who had been working turned to play, and all who had been playing gave themselves joyfully to work. Those who had been singing, and making melody on different instruments, fell silent and began to listen. Those who had been walking alone in meditation met together in companies to talk. And those who had been far away on errands to the Earth and other planets came homeward like a flight of swallows to the high cliff when the day is over.

It was not that they needed to be restored from weariness, for the inhabitants of that country never say, "I am tired." But there, as here, the law of change is the secret of happiness, and the joy that never ends is woven of mingled strands of labour and repose, society and solitude, music and silence. Sleep comes to them not as it does to us, with a darkening of the vision and a folding of the wings of the spirit, but with an opening of the eyes to deeper and fuller light, and with an effortless outgoing of the soul upon broader currents of life, as the sun-loving bird poises and circles upward, without a wing-beat, on the upholding air.

It was in one of the quiet corners of the green valley called Peacefield, where the little brook of Brighthopes runs smoothly down to join the River of Life, that I saw a company of angels, returned from various labours on Earth, sitting in friendly converse on the hill-side, where cyclamens and arbutus and violets and fringed orchids and pale lady's-tresses, and all the sweet-smelling flowers which are separated in the lower world by the seasons, were thrown together in a harmony of fragrance. There were three of the company who seemed to be leaders, distinguished not only by more radiant and powerful looks, but by a tone of authority in their speech and by the willing attention with which the others listened to them, as they talked of their earthly tasks, of the tangles and troubles, the wars and miseries that they had seen among men, and of the best way to get rid of them and bring sorrow to an end.

"The Earth is full of oppression and unrighteousness," said the tallest and most powerful of the angels. His voice was deep and strong, and by his shining armour and the long two-handed sword hanging over his shoulder I knew that he was the archangel Michael, the mightiest one among the warriors of the King, and the executor of the divine judgments upon the unjust. "The Earth is tormented with injustice," he cried, "and the great misery that I have seen among men is that the evil hand is often stronger than the good hand and can beat it down.

"The arm of the cruel is heavier than the arm of the kind. The unjust get the better of the just and tread on them. I have seen tyrant kings crush their helpless folk. I have seen the fields of the innocent trampled into bloody ruin by the feet of conquering armies. I have seen the wicked nation overcome the peoples that loved liberty, and take away their treasure by force of arms. I have seen poverty mocked by arrogant wealth, and purity deflowered by brute violence, and gentleness and fair-dealing bruised in the winepress of iniquity and pride.

"There is no cure for this evil, but by the giving of greater force to the good hand. The righteous cause must be strengthened with might to resist the wicked, to defend the helpless, to punish all cruelty and unfairness, to uphold the right everywhere, and to enforce justice with unconquerable arms. Oh, that the host of Heaven might be called, arrayed, and sent to mingle in the wars of men, to make the good victorious, to destroy all evil, and to make the will of the King prevail!

"We would shake down the thrones of tyrants, and loose the bands of the oppressed. We would hold the cruel and violent with the bit of fear, and drive the greedy and fierce-minded men with the whip of terror. We would stand guard, with weapons drawn, about the innocent, the gentle, the kind, and keep the peace of God with the sword of the angels!"

As he spoke, his hands were lifted to the hilt of his long blade, and he raised it above him, straight and shining, throwing sparkles of light around it, like the spray from the sharp prow of a moving ship. Bright flames of heavenly ardour leaped in the eyes of the listening angels; a martial air passed over their faces as if they longed for the call to war.

But no silver trumpet blared from the battlements of the City of God; no crimson flag was unfurled on those high, secret walls; no thrilling drum-beat echoed over the smooth meadow. Only the sound of the brook of Brighthopes was heard tinkling and murmuring among the roots of the grasses and flowers; and far off a cadence of song drifted down from the inner courts of the Palace of the King.

Then another angel began to speak, and made answer to Michael. He, too, was tall and wore the look of power. But it was power of the mind rather than of the hand. His face was clear and glistening, and his eyes were lit with a steady flame which neither leaped nor fell. Of flame also were his garments, which clung about him as the fire enwraps a torch burning where there is no wind; and his great wings, spiring to a point far above his head, were like a living lamp before the altar of the Most High. By this sign I knew that it was the archangel Uriel, the spirit of the Sun, clearest in vision, deepest in wisdom of all the spirits that surround the throne.

"I hold not the same thought," said he, "as the great archangel Michael; nor, though I desire the same end which he desires, would I seek it by the same way. For I know how often power has been given to the good, and how often it has been turned aside and used for evil. I know that the host of Heaven, and the very stars in their courses, have fought on the side of a favoured nation; yet pride has followed triumph and oppression has been the first-born child of victory. I know that the deliverers of the people have become tyrants over those whom they have set free, and the fighters for liberty have been changed into the soldiers of fortune. Power corrupts itself, and might cannot save.

"Does not the Prince Michael remember how the angel of the Lord led the armies of Israel, and gave them the battle against every foe, except the enemy within the camp? And how they robbed and crushed the peoples against whom they had fought for freedom? And how the wickedness of the tribes of Canaan survived their conquest and overcame their conquerors, so that the children of Israel learned to worship the idols of their enemies, Moloch, and Baal, and Ashtoreth?

"Power corrupts itself, and might cannot save. Was not Persia the destroyer of Babylon, and did not the tyranny of Persia cry aloud for destruction? Did not Rome break the yoke of the East, and does not the yoke of Rome lie heavy on the shoulders of the world? Listen!"

There was silence for a moment on the slopes of Peacefield, and then over the encircling hills a cool wind brought the sound of chains clanking in prisons and galleys, the sighing of millions of slaves, the weeping of wretched women and children, the blows of hammers nailing men to their crosses. Then the sound passed by with the wind, and Uriel spoke again:

"Power corrupts itself, and might cannot save. The Earth is full of ignorant strife, and for this evil there is no cure but by the giving of greater knowledge. It is because men do not understand evil that they yield themselves to its power. Wickedness is folly in action, and injustice is the error of the blind. It is because men are ignorant that they destroy one another, and at last themselves.

"If there were more light in the world there would be no sorrow. If the great King who knows all things would enlighten the world with wisdom—wisdom to understand his law and his ways, to read the secrets of the earth and the stars, to discern the workings of the heart of man and the things that make for joy and peace—if he would but send us, his messengers, as a flame of fire to shine upon those who sit in darkness, how gladly would we go to bring in the new day!

"We would speak the word of warning and counsel to the erring, and tell knowledge to the perplexed. We would guide the ignorant in the paths of prudence, and the young would sit at our feet and hear us gladly in the school of life. Then folly would fade away as the morning vapour, and the sun of wisdom would shine on all men, and the peace of God would come with the counsel of the angels."

A murmur of pleasure followed the words of Uriel, and eager looks flashed around the circle of the messengers of light as they heard the praise of wisdom fitly spoken. But there was one among them on whose face a shadow of doubt rested, and though he smiled, it was as if he remembered something that the others had forgotten. He turned to an angel near him.

"Who was it," said he, "to whom you were sent with counsel long ago? Was it not Balaam the son of Beor, as he was riding to meet the King of Moab? And did not even the dumb beast profit more by your instruction than the man who rode him? And who was it," he continued, turning to Uriel, "that was called the wisest of all men, having searched out and understood the many inventions that are found under the sun? Was not Solomon, prince of fools and philosophers, unable by much learning to escape weariness of the flesh and despair of the spirit? Knowledge also is vanity and vexation. This I know well, because I have dwelt among men and held converse with them since the day when I was sent to instruct the first man in Eden."

Then I looked more closely at him who was speaking and recognised the beauty of the archangel Raphael, as it was pictured long ago:

> *"A seraph winged; six wings he wore to shade*
> *His lineaments divine; the pair that clad*
> *Each shoulder broad came mantling o'er his breast,*
> *With regal ornament; the middle pair*
> *Girt like a starry zone his waist, and round*
> *Skirted his loins and thighs with downy gold*
> *And colours dipped in Heav'n; the third his feet*
> *Shadowed from either heel with feathered mail,*
> *Sky-tinctured grain. Like Maia's son he stood*
> *And shook his plumes, that Heavenly fragrance filled*
> *The circuit wide."*

"Too well I know," he spoke on, while the smile on his face deepened into a look of pity and tenderness and desire, "too well I know that power corrupts itself and that knowledge cannot save. There is no cure for the evil that is in the world but by the giving of more love to men. The laws that are ordained for earth are strange and unequal, and the ways where men must walk are full of pitfalls and dangers. Pestilence creeps along the ground and flows in the rivers; whirlwind and tempest shake the habitations of men and drive their ships to destruction; fire breaks forth from the mountains and the foundations of the world tremble. Frail is the flesh of man, and many are his pains and troubles. His children can never find peace until they learn to love one another and to help one another.

"Wickedness is begotten by disease and misery. Violence comes from poverty and hunger. The cruelty of oppression is when the strong tread the weak under their feet; the bitterness of pride is when the wise and learned despise the simple; the crown of folly is when the rich think they are gods, and the poor think that God is not.

"Hatred and envy and contempt are the curse of life. And for these there is no remedy save love—the will to give and to bless—the will of the King himself, who gives to all and is loving unto every man. But how shall the hearts of men be won to this will? How shall it enter into them and possess them? Even the gods that men fashion for themselves are cruel and proud and false and unjust. How shall the miracle be wrought in human nature to reveal the meaning of humanity? How shall men be made like God?"

At this question a deep hush fell around the circle, and every listener was still, even as the rustling leaves hang motionless when the light breeze falls away in the hour of sunset. Then through the silence, like the song of a far-away thrush from its hermitage in the forest, a voice came ringing: "I know it, I know it, I know it."

Clear and sweet—clear as a ray of light, sweeter than the smallest silver bell that rang the hour of rest—was that slender voice floating on the odorous and translucent air. Nearer and nearer it came, echoing down the valley, "I know it, I know it, I know it!"

Then from between the rounded hills, among which the brook of Brighthopes is born, appeared a young angel, a little child, with flying hair of gold, and green wreaths twined about his shoulders, and fluttering hands that played upon the air and seemed to lift him so lightly that he had no need of wings. As thistle-down, blown by the wind, dances across the water, so he came along the little stream, singing clear above the murmur of the brook.

All the angels rose and turned to look at him with wondering eyes. Multitudes of others came flying swiftly to the place from which the strange, new song was sounding. Rank within rank, like a garden of living flowers, they stood along the sloping banks of the brook while the child-angel floated into the midst of them, singing:

"I know it, I know it, I know it! Man shall be made like God because the Son of God shall become a man."

At this all the angels looked at one another with amazement, and gathered more closely about the child-angel, as those who hear wonderful news.

"How can this be?" they asked. "How is it possible that the Son of God should be a man?"

"I do not know," said the young angel. "I only know that it is to be."

"But if he becomes a man," said Raphael, "he will be at the mercy of men; the cruel and the wicked will have power upon him; he will suffer."

"I know it," answered the young angel, "and by suffering he will understand the meaning of all sorrow and pain; and he will be able to comfort every one who cries; and his own tears will be for the healing of sad hearts; and those who are healed by him will learn for his sake to be kind to each other."

"But if the Son of God is a true man," said Uriel, "he must first be a child, simple, and lowly, and helpless. It may be that he will never gain the learning of the schools. The masters of earthly wisdom will despise him and speak scorn of him."

"I know it," said the young angel, "but in meekness will he answer them; and to those who become as little children he will give the heavenly wisdom that comes, without seeking, to the pure and gentle of heart."

"But if he becomes a man," said Michael, "evil men will hate and persecute him: they may even take his life, if they are stronger than he."

"I know it," answered the young angel, "they will nail him to a cross. But when he is lifted up, he will draw all men unto him, for he will still be the Son of God, and no heart that is open to love can help loving him, since his love for men is so great that he is willing to die for them."

"But how do you know these things?" cried the other angels. "Who are you?"

"I am the Christmas angel," he said. "At first I was sent as the dream of a little child, a holy child, blessed and wonderful, to dwell in the heart of a pure virgin, Mary of Nazareth. There I was hidden till the word came to call me back to the throne of the King, and tell me my name, and give me my new message. For this is Christmas day on Earth, and to-day the Son of God is born of a woman. So I must fly quickly, before the sun rises, to bring the good news to those happy men who have been chosen to receive them."

As he said this, the young angel rose, with arms outspread, from the green meadow of Peacefield and, passing over the bounds of Heaven, dropped swiftly as a shooting-star toward the night shadow of the Earth. The other angels followed him—a throng of dazzling forms, beautiful as a rain of jewels falling from the dark-blue sky. But the child-angel went more swiftly than the others, because of the certainty of gladness in his heart.

And as the others followed him they wondered who had been favoured and chosen to receive the glad tidings.

"It must be the Emperor of the World and his counsellors," they thought. But the flight passed over Rome.

"It may be the philosophers and the masters of learning," they thought. But the flight passed over Athens.

"Can it be the High Priest of the Jews, and the elders and the scribes?" they thought. But the flight passed over Jerusalem.

It floated out over the hill country of Bethlehem; the throng of silent angels holding close together, as if perplexed and doubtful; the child-angel darting on far in advance, as one who knew the way through the darkness.

The villages were all still: the very houses seemed asleep; but in one place there was a low sound of talking in a stable, near to an inn—a sound as of a mother soothing her baby to rest.

All over the pastures on the hillsides a light film of snow had fallen, delicate as the veil of a bride adorned for the marriage; and as the child-angel passed over them, alone in the swiftness of his flight, the pure fields sparkled round him, giving back his radiance.

And there were in that country shepherds abiding in the fields, keeping watch over their flocks by night. And lo! the angel of the Lord came upon them, and the glory of the Lord shone round about them, and they were sore afraid. And the angel said unto them: "Fear not; for behold I bring you glad tidings of great joy which shall be to all nations. For unto you is born this day, in the city of David, a Saviour, which is Christ the Lord. And this shall be a sign unto you; ye shall find the babe wrapped in swaddling clothes, lying in a manger."

And suddenly there was with the angel a multitude of the heavenly host, praising God and saying: "Glory to God in the highest, and on earth peace, good-will toward men." And the shepherds said one to another: "Let us now go, even to Bethlehem, and see this thing which is come to pass."

So I said within myself that I also would go with the shepherds, even to Bethlehem. And I heard a great and sweet voice, as of a bell, which said, "Come!" And when the bell had sounded twelve times, I awoke; and it was Christmas morn; and I knew that I had been in a dream.

Yet it seemed to me that the things which I had heard were true.

A Little Essay

Christmas-Giving and Christmas-Living

I

The custom of exchanging presents on a certain day in the year is very much older than Christmas, and means very much less. It has obtained in almost all ages of the world, and among many different nations. It is a fine thing or a foolish thing, as the case may be; an encouragement to friendliness, or a tribute to fashion; an expression of good nature, or a bid for favour; an outgoing of generosity, or a disguise of greed; a cheerful old custom, or a futile old farce, according to the spirit which animates it and the form which it takes.

But when this ancient and variously interpreted tradition of a day of gifts was transferred to the Christmas season, it was brought into vital contact with an idea which must transform it, and with an example which must lift it up to a higher plane. The example is the life of Jesus. The idea is unselfish interest in the happiness of others.

The great gift of Jesus to the world was himself. He lived with and for men. He kept back nothing. In every particular and personal gift that he made to certain people there was something of himself that made it precious.

For example, at the wedding in Cana of Galilee, it was his thought for the feelings of the giver of the feast, and his wish that every guest should find due entertainment, that lent the flavour of a heavenly hospitality to the wine which he provided.

When he gave bread and fish to the hungry multitude who had followed him out among the hills by the Lake of Gennesaret, the people were refreshed and strengthened by the sense of the personal care of Jesus for their welfare, as much as by the food which he bestowed upon them. It was another illustration of the sweetness of "a dinner of herbs, where love is."

The gifts of healing which he conferred upon many different kinds of sufferers were, in every case, evidences that Jesus was willing to give something of himself, his thought, his sympathy, his vital power, to the men and women among whom he lived. Once, when a paralytic was brought to Jesus on a bed, he surprised everybody, and offended many, by giving the poor wretch the pardon of his sins, before he gave new life to his body. That was just because Jesus thought before he gave; because he desired to satisfy the deepest need; because in fact he gave something of himself in every gift. All true Christmas-giving ought to be after this pattern.

Not that it must all be solemn and serious. For the most part it deals with little wants, little joys, little tokens of friendly feeling. But the feeling must be more than the token; else the gift does not really belong to Christmas.

It takes time and effort and unselfish expenditure of strength to make gifts in this way. But it is the only way that fits the season.

The finest Christmas gift is not the one that costs the most money, but the one that carries the most love.

II

But how seldom Christmas comes—only once a year; and how soon it is over—a night and a day! If that is the whole of it, it seems not much more durable than the little toys that one buys of a fakir on the street-corner. They run for an hour, and then the spring breaks, and the legs come off, and nothing remains but a contribution to the dust heap.

But surely that need not and ought not to be the whole of Christmas—only [pg 38] a single day of generosity, ransomed from the dull servitude of a selfish year,—only a single night of merry-making, celebrated in the slave-quarters of a selfish race! If every gift is the token of a personal thought, a friendly feeling, an unselfish interest in the joy of others, then the thought, the feeling, the interest, may remain after the gift is made.

The little present, or the rare and long-wished-for gift (it matters not whether the vessel be of gold, or silver, or iron, or wood, or clay, or just a small bit of birch bark folded into a cup), may carry a message something like this:

"I am thinking of you to-day, because it is Christmas, and I wish you happiness. And to-morrow, because it will be the day after Christmas, I shall still wish you happiness; and so on, clear through the year. I may not be able to tell you about it every day, because I may be far away; or because both of us may be very busy; or perhaps because I cannot even afford to pay the postage on so many letters, or find the time to write them. But that makes no difference. The thought and the wish will be here just the same. In my work and in the business of life, I mean to try not to be unfair to you or injure you in any way. In my pleasure, if we can be together, I would like to share the fun with you. Whatever joy or success comes to you will make me glad. Without pretense, and in plain words, good-will to you is what I mean, in the Spirit of Christmas."

It is not necessary to put a message like this into high-flown language, to swear absolute devotion and deathless consecration. In love and friendship, small, steady payments on a gold basis are better than immense promissory notes. Nor, indeed, is it always necessary to put the message into words at all, nor even to convey it by a tangible token. To feel it and to act it out—that is the main thing.

There are a great many people in the world whom we know more or less, but to whom for various reasons we cannot very well send a Christmas gift. But there is hardly one, in all the circles of our acquaintance, with whom we may not exchange the touch of Christmas life.

In the outer circles, cheerful greetings, courtesy, consideration; in the inner circles, sympathetic interest, hearty congratulations, honest encouragement; in the inmost circle, comradeship, helpfulness, tenderness,—

"Beautiful friendship tried by sun and wind
Durable from the daily dust of life."

After all, Christmas-living is the best kind of Christmas-giving.

A Short Christmas Sermon

Keeping Christmas

Romans, xiv, 6: He that regardeth the day, regardeth it unto the Lord.

It is a good thing to observe Christmas day. The mere marking of times and seasons, when men agree to stop work and make merry together, is a wise and wholesome custom. It helps one to feel the supremacy of the common life over the individual life. It reminds a man to set his own little watch, now and then, by the great clock of humanity which runs on sun time.

But there is a better thing than the observance of Christmas day, and that is, keeping Christmas.

Are you willing to forget what you have done for other people, and to remember what other people have done for you; to ignore what the world owes you, and to think what you owe the world; to put your rights in the background, and your duties in the middle distance, and your chances to do a little more than your duty in the foreground; to see that your fellow-men are just as real as you are, and try to look behind their faces to their hearts, hungry for joy; to own that probably the only good reason for your existence is not what you are going to get out of life, but what you are going to give to life; to close your book of complaints against the management of the universe, and look around you for a place where you can sow a few seeds of happiness—are you willing to do these things even for a day? Then you can keep Christmas.

Are you willing to stoop down and consider the needs and the desires of little children; to remember the weakness and loneliness of people who are growing old; to stop asking how much your friends love you, and ask yourself whether you love them enough; to bear in mind the things that other people have to bear on their hearts; to try to understand what those who live in the same house with you really want, without waiting for them to tell you; to trim your lamp so that it will give more light and less smoke, and to carry it in front so that your shadow will fall behind you; to make a grave for your ugly thoughts, and a garden for your kindly feelings, with the gate open—are you willing to do these things even for a day? Then you can keep Christmas.

Are you willing to believe that love is the strongest thing in the world—stronger than hate, stronger than evil, stronger than death—and that the blessed life which began in Bethlehem nineteen hundred years ago is the image and brightness of the Eternal Love? Then you can keep Christmas.

And if you keep it for a day, why not always?

But you can never keep it alone.

Two Christmas Prayers

A Christmas Prayer for the Home

Father of all men, look upon our
>family,
Kneeling together before Thee,
And grant us a true Christmas.

With loving heart we bless Thee:
For the gift of Thy dear Son
>Jesus Christ,
For the peace He brings to human
>homes,
For the good-will He teaches to
>sinful men,
For the glory of Thy goodness
>shining in His face.

With joyful voice we praise Thee:
For His lowly birth and His rest
    in the manger,
For the pure tenderness of His
    mother Mary,
For the fatherly care that
    protected Him,
For the Providence that saved the
    Holy Child
To be the Saviour of the world.

With deep desire we beseech Thee:
Help us to keep His birthday
    truly,
Help us to offer, in His name, our
    Christmas prayer.

From the sickness of sin and the
    darkness of doubt,
From selfish pleasures and sullen
    pains,

From the frost of pride and the fever
    of envy,

God save us every one, through the
    blessing of Jesus.
In the health of purity and the calm
    of mutual trust,
In the sharing of joy and the bearing
    of trouble,
In the steady glow of love and the
    clear light of hope,
God keep us every one, by the
    blessing of Jesus.

In praying and praising, in giving
    and receiving,
In eating and drinking, in singing
    and making merry,
In parents' gladness and in children's
    mirth,
In dear memories of those who have
    departed,

In good comradeship with those who
    are here,
In kind wishes for those who are far
    away,

In patient waiting, sweet contentment,
    generous cheer,
God bless us every one, with the
    blessing of Jesus.

By remembering our kinship with all
    men,
By well-wishing, friendly speaking and
    kindly doing,
By cheering the downcast and adding
    sunshine to daylight,
By welcoming strangers (poor
    shepherds or wise men),
By keeping the music of the angels'
    song in this home,
God help us every one to share the
    blessing of Jesus:

In whose name we keep
    Christmas:
And in whose words we
    pray together:

Our Father which art in heaven, hallowed be
   Thy name.
Thy kingdom come. Thy will be done in
   earth, as it is in heaven.
Give us this day our daily bread. And forgive us
   our debts, as we forgive our debtors.
And lead us not into temptation, but deliver us
   from evil:
For Thine is the kingdom, and the power,
   and the glory, forever. Amen.

A Christmas Prayer for Lonley Folks

Lord God of the solitary,
Look upon me in my loneliness.
Since I may not keep this Christmas
    in the home,
Send it into my heart.

Let not my sins cloud me in,
But shine through them with
    forgiveness in the face of
    the child Jesus.

Put me in loving remembrance of
    the lowly lodging in the
    stable of Bethlehem,

The sorrows of the blessed Mary, the poverty and exile of the Prince of Peace.
For His sake, give me a cheerful courage to endure my lot,
And an inward comfort to sweeten it.

Purge my heart from hard and bitter thoughts.
Let no shadow of forgetting come between me and friends far away:
Bless them in their Christmas mirth:
Hedge me in with faithfulness,
That I may not grow unworthy to meet them again.

Give me good work to do,
That I may forget myself and find peace in doing it for Thee.
Though I am poor, send me to carry some gift to those who are poorer,

Some cheer to those who are more
    lonely.
Grant me the joy to do a kindness
    to one of Thy little ones:
Light my Christmas candle at the
    gladness of an innocent and
    grateful heart.
Strange is the path where Thou
    leadest me:
Let me not doubt Thy wisdom, nor
    lose Thy hand.
Make me sure that Eternal Love is
    revealed in Jesus, Thy dear
    Son,
To save us from sin and solitude and
    death.
Teach me that I am not alone,
But that many hearts, all round the
    world,
Join with me through the silence,
while I pray in His name:

Our Father which art in heaven, hallowed be Thy name.

Thy kingdom come. Thy will be done in earth, as it is in heaven.

Give us this day our daily bread. And forgive us our debts, as we forgive our debtors.

And lead us not into temptation, but deliver us from evil:

For Thine is the kingdom, and the power, and the glory, forever. Amen.

www.ingramcontent.com/pod-product-compliance
Lightning Source LLC
Chambersburg PA
CBHW071649040426
42452CB00009B/1813